Table of Contents

c. How to How to tell that your Yorkshire Terrier is on heat?

d. Yorkie Pregnancy Signs

e. Care for the Yorkie during pregnancy

f. The labour and delivery process

g. Care for Yorkie and puppies post-delivery

6. Spaying and Neutering

a. Benefits of spaying and neutering

b. Recommended age

c. Will it affect my Yorkie's personality or behaviour?

7. The Senior Years

a. Signs of aging

b. Taking care of a senior Yorkie

1

History and Introduction of the Yorkshire Terrier

The Yorkshire Terrier (also popularly known as the Yorkie), as the name suggests, originates from Yorkshire, a region in the north of England in the mid of the 19th century. It used to be bred to help farmers in catching rats and other rodents in clothing mills due to its natural hunter instincts. The Yorkshire Terrier today is now kept as a toy dog in families.

Characteristics of the Yorkshire Terrier

The Yorkie is one of the smallest breeds in the dog population. It weighs typically between 4 to 7 pounds and ranges from 6 to 9 inches tall at the shoulders. Though small, they tend to think big. Yorkshire Terriers are not afraid of mixing around with dogs of sizes much larger than them. In fact, they are highly sociable and would seek friendship with them. It is not surprising to witness Yorkshire Terriers voluntarily approaching the big dogs wanting to play with them. The Yorkshire Terrier is an energetic and playful dog who is curious and affectionate. They make perfect and lovable companions for both adults and children.

Yorkshire Terriers tend enjoy barking in nature. However, they can be trained as a puppy to control or tame their barking. In fact, there are

Yorkshires that have been trained not to bark since young so much so that they can be kept in a bag to travel in buses and trains with no one knowing that a dog is on board!

The Yorkie as a companion for kids

Yorkshire Terriers get along well with kids. However, it is best that kids are supervised by parents when they play with the Yorkie, as kids have the tendency to create mental stress or trauma for the dog by pulling its hair or grabbing its body.

Although the Yorkie belongs to a breed that does not shed, parents need to be mindful that its hair or saliva can still be a trigger for asthma or eczema if a child suffers from these conditions. It is best that the child avoids touching or getting too near to the Yorkie before the child's lungs are strong enough to be resistant to such allergies.

The Yorkie's Coat

The Yorkshire Terrier has a rich black coat on its body and a rich bright tan on its face and limbs as a puppy. As the Yorkie grows with age, usually after one year, the tan lightens and darkness of the body black coat will fade to a greyish tint.

A Yorkshire Puppy   An adult Yorkshire Terrier

Adult Yorkshire Terriers that participate in dog shows would have their hair kept long to display their coat colour, quality and texture. Show quality Yorkies should have their hair shiny, fine, smooth, and straight.

Long-haired Yorkies would require regular brushing and maintenance.

Health of the Yorkie

Given its small size, Yorkshire Terriers can stay active indoors. However, it is always beneficial to the Yorkie's health if it can be brought for a short walk or run outdoors to enjoy the spaciousness and greenery of the natural environment.

The average lifespan of a Yorkshire Terrier is about 15 to 16 years. However, it has been known that small dogs tend to be able to live longer. If in good health, it is possible that Yorkies can live for as long as 20 years or more. It is important for Yorkies to be checked by the vet and be immunized against common diseases on an annual basis.

2

The Yorkshire Terrier Puppy

How to choose a Yorkie Puppy?

Visit a reputable breeder when considering your purchase of a Yorkie puppy. It is necessary to ensure that the puppy is of at least 8 weeks of age when you make the purchase to be in compliance with US regulations. Puppies that are less than 8 weeks will be extremely vulnerable may not know how to feed itself properly.

A healthy puppy should be curious, lively and loves to play. Observe its behavior when placed together with its litter of siblings. If the puppy displays signs of anxiety, aggressiveness and fear, it could pose a problem in its behavior when being kept as your pet.

Check that its eyes are brightly black, its ears and nose are clean and its hair looks healthy and shiny. Any symptoms of cough or runny nose or excessive discharge observed could mean that the puppy is not in a good state of health. Perform a simple hearing test to check if the puppy responds to sound.

Once you have selected the puppy of your choice, check its birth and related documentation and that it contains the necessary clauses to protect your rights. (e.g. the return of the puppy/refund should the puppy be found to be sick within X number of hours). If it has not been given the DHPP and vaccine against rabies and other common diseases, as well as be treated for heartworm and other common parasites, it will be a priority task for you to bring it to the vet for vaccination once it becomes your pet.

Feeding your Yorkie puppy

Yorkies do not have a big appetite and this is especially so for young Yorkies. Hence, it would be best to distribute its meals to 3 times a day, of which 2 of its daily meals could consist of dry foods. You can include some dry foods that consist of lamb meat as they contribute to the Yorkie's health and bring shine to the Yorkie's coat. Treats can be considered a meal but do not overfeed on treats as your Yorkie may not be getting a balanced diet from excessive treats.

Yorkies love milk and cheese. You can give them in moderation but if they were to suffer an upset stomach as a result, stop feeding the milk and consult the doctor if it is suitable to continue having milk in their diet.

If you plan to change their diet, do so gradually over 2-3 weeks such that their stomachs can be accustomed to the changes. Sudden changes in diet may cause vomiting and diarrhea due to an upset stomach.

Forbidden Foods

Foods that are delicacies to the humans may turn out to be poisonous to Yorkies and other dogs. Please be very careful in selecting the foods and treats for your Yorkie.

Please take note that they following foods should never be given to your dog and take caution that your Yorkie has no chance to get near them.

• Chocolates and cocoa
The ingredient "theobromine" found in chocolate is toxic to dogs and can cause fatalities when consumed. Please ensure that any chocolate or cocoa-containing tidbit or snack is not given to your Yorkie.

• Grapes and raisins
Although beneficial to the human body, grapes and raisins can cause a fatal damage to a dog's kidneys.

• Alcohol

As in humans, dogs can also suffer from alcohol-poisoning.

• Sugar-free foods
The artificial sweetener xylitol contained in sugar-free items can cause the blood-sugar to drop adversely in a dog which can result in coordination loss and seizures. When in doubt if a food is sugar-free, do avoid feeding it to your dog.

• Nuts
Nuts, especially macadamia should not be given to your dog as they contain high phosphorus that can impede the limb movements or even paralyse your Yorkie.

• Raw Eggs
Raw eggs cannot be easily absorbed by the dog's body and may result in indigestion and an upset stomach.

• Fatty Foods
Do not over feed your Yorkie with fatty dogs such as chicken skin as they may cause a burden to the pancreas of your dog. Such foods that are detrimental to the human health are also not advisable for your dog for the obvious reasons.

• Food for another animal's diet
Food meant for another pet such as cat food should not be used to feed your Yorkie as the amount of proteins contained in cat foods may be too excessive for a dog's body to tolerate.

• Hard bones
Soft bones can serve as a delicious treat for your dog. Hard bones like those from the chicken can be very sharp and may hurt or cause damages to your Yorkie's throat and stomach and should not be given to your Yorkie.

• Salty foods
Similar to the effects of excessive salt in humans, dogs should not be given food that contain too much salt as they may result in hair loss due to dehydration.

Toilet Training

House training will take a while for a while and much patience will be required before a Yorkie puppy can be effectively toilet-trained. The use of dog pee sheets/pads are recommended as they are highly absorbent and would be able to help keep your Yorkie's legs dry and clean.

The pee sheets can also serve as reminder for your Yorkie that it can only pee or poo on this sheet in the house and nowhere else.

Dog Pee Sheets

If your Yorkie was to pee elsewhere, always guide it to the sheet immediately after its "offence" and correct it promptly. If your Yorkie puppy were to litter in the right place, praise it abundantly and offer it with treats.

You may also like to schedule your Yorkie's toilet sessions by guiding it to the sheet after every meal if possible. Younger puppies may require more frequent potty sessions like once every 2 hours. Associate its potty session with a word or phrase repeatedly such that it can relate it accordingly when the word is mentioned.

A crate can be used if you are unable to supervise your Yorkie. Your Yorkie may feel more secure in the crate and would less likely urinate while in the crate. However, do not leave puppies in the crate for more than 3 hours and more than 7 hours for an adult Yorkie. They would require their potty breaks when let out of their crate. The same potty training would apply.

Your Yorkie will be eventually house-trained with your time and patience in educating it the right way.

Training a Yorkie not to bark

Yorkshire Terriers love to bark in nature. But they can be trained not to bark unnecessarily from young.

If your Yorkie is barking for the wrong reason, stop it with an assertive tone and word or phrase. E.g. "Quiet", "No" or "Stop the barking". If just this does not work, you can attempt some forms of mild punishment, such as spraying your Yorkie's face with water using a water pistol whenever it is barking inappropriately. If all else fail to work, you can consider the use of a "no-bark" collar. However, this should only be the last resort as it may result in the dog to suffer from emotional trauma.

3

Grooming

Popular Yorkie Grooming Styles

Depending on your preference and your Yorkie's hygiene conditions, the following are some popular grooming styles of Yorkshire Terriers:

<u>Modified Westie Cut</u>

The modified Westie Cut is a Yorkie cut that is modified from the haircut of that of a Westie. The face is shaped round and the ears trimmed to stand pointed. Hair on the body and stomach is trimmed short and hair around the legs is given a longer length.

Modified Westie Cut

<u>Puppy Cut</u>

The puppy cut is short with the face and entire body trimmed to give the dog a young look. This would be an ideal cut for owners who prefer better manageability in maintaining the hair of their Yorkies. Only light brushing would be needed.

Puppy Cut

Schnauzer Cut

The Schnauzer cut is a popular and trendy cut and owners can opt for this cut for their Yorkies to make them look like Schnauzers. The face is shaped longish to give it a beard-like appearance.

Schnauzer Cut

Long Coat

The long coat would be a natural choice if you have plans to enter your Yorkie in competitions. Regular combing and brushing would be needs to prevent its hair from being entangled. You may also require to shower your Yorkie more often for hygiene reasons.

Long Coat

Trimming your Yorkie's nails

It is best to take your Yorkie to the groomer to have its nails trimmed. But if you decide to trim them yourself, do purchase a nail clipper designed for dogs from the pet shop. When trimming your Yorkie's nails, hold your dog's paws firmly and be careful to only trim the outer nail shell outside the kwik, shown in the shaded area below. Accidental cutting of the kwik will result and pain and bleeding of your Yorkie as it contains numerous veins and blood vessels.

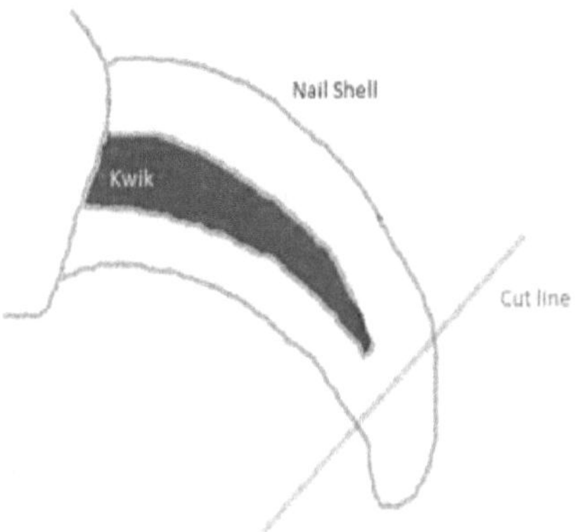

Cleaning your Yorkie's teeth

Due to the structure of the Yorkie's teeth and narrow jaws, plaque can build up easily, resulting in tooth decay and gum diseases. As such, it is necessary that your Yorkie's teeth are cleaned regularly.

The choice of the toothbrush for a Yorkie is important. Choose a toothbrush that is designed for small breeds to effective brush its teeth including the difficult to reach areas. These toothbrushes are readily available at the pet supplies stores.

Also choose a toothpaste that has a flavor that your dog is comfortable with. Never use a human toothpaste for your Yorkie as it contains fluoride that is toxic to dogs.

Be patient when first attempting to brush your Yorkie's teeth. Tilt your

Yorkie's head firmly and gently secure a good grip such that its mouth is opened wide enough to introduce the toothbrush. Use circular motions in the brushing process to clean both the inner and outer teeth. Keep it short for a start until your Yorkie gets accustomed to this routine and you can brush its teeth more thoroughly.

It would be ideal to brush your Yorkie's teeth daily but if it is resistant to brushing, try to brush its teeth at least once a week.

Other alternatives would be to use dental wipes, dental sprays, treats or chewing toys that can help clean your Yorkie's teeth.

It would be advisable to send your Yorkie for dental treatment at the vet once a year. It would be treated under general anesthesia where its teeth would be thoroughly cleaned and decayed tooth would be extracted during the procedure.

Cleaning your Yorkie's ears

It is necessary to clean your Yorkie's ears to remove any wax or dirt build up as well as to prevent any infections. Ear cleaning can be done once a week after showering your Yorkie.

The process for cleaning your Yorkie's ears would be as follows:

i)   Remove excess hair by plucking them out using tweezers. Excess hair accumulated can hamper the flow of air into the ear canal leasing to moisture build up.

ii)   Dab some ear cleaning solution (purchased from your vet or pet supplies store) on a cotton ball or swab and gently wipe the insides of the ear. Avoid introducing it too deep into the ears as it can puncture its ear drums.

Your Yorkie's ears may be infected if you see any redness or swelling, or notice any foul odour from its ears. If this happens, do not attempt to clean it ears. Bring it to the vet for further examination and treatment if needed.

4

Health Issues

Common medical conditions in Yorkies, symptoms and treatments

Yorkshire Terriers are prone to medical conditions related to their digestive systems such as vomiting and diarrhea and hence owners need to administer their diet with care.

The following are some common medical conditions, symptoms in Yorkies and their treatments which would be useful to note.

Hypoglycemia (low-blood sugar)
A serious condition where blood sugar levels drop drastically. It is common for Yorkshire Terrier puppies up to 4 months old but it may happen to some adult Yorkies.

Symptoms: Drowsiness, shivering, fainting, confusion, seizures, disorientation, weakness in response and movement, depression, tremors, a drop in body temperature, and even coma.

Treatment: Give it some honey if it can still consume and bring your Yorkie to the vet if you notice any these symptoms, especially with a drop in body temperature.

Liver Shunt

A potentially fatal congenital condition in which the blood bypasses the liver. Some unfortunate Yorkies are born with this condition where the toxins get built up in the Yorkie's blood.

Symptoms: Little weight gain, digestive problems, persistent thirst, problems with urinary system, lack of energy, depression, disorientated movement, seizures following a meal.

Treatment: Medication and diet may help in giving temporary relief but its liver will eventually fail if surgery is not performed to restore blood flow. However, the surgery comes with significant risks and some Yorkies may die from the surgery.

Hemorrhagic Gastroenteritis (HGE)

A form of diarrhea that can be life threatening.

Symptoms: Bloody or mucous- covered stools, persistent diarrhea, vomiting, loss of appetite.

Treatment: Excessive dehydration of the Yorkie may endanger its life. If the diarrhea or vomiting persists and is affecting your Yorkie's ability to function normally, bring it to seek a vet's attention immediately.

Collapsing Trachea

A condition where the cartilage weakens and airflow into a Yorkie's lungs gets affected, which can result in a chronic dry cough, breathlessness or fainting.

Symptoms: In addition to a disturbing cough, other symptoms include difficulty in breathing and a bluish tinge seen on the gums.

Treatment: A series of tests need to be conducted before this condition can be confirmed by the vet. Common treatments would be cough suppressants, bronchodilators and corticosteroids or antibiotics if inflammation is present. Surgery may be recommended if the common treatment methods fail to work.

Legg-Perthes Disease

A disease of the hip joint which may affect some young Yorkies less than 12 months of age where its hip area is not receiving inadequate circulation of blood, resulting in the bone in the dog's femur to weaken. The cartilage surrounding this may crack.

Symptoms: Limping and pain. The condition can only be confirmed by an X-ray. Repeated X-rays over time may be required due to the show changes of the bone.

Treatment: Surgery is the only option to remove the damaged head and neck of the hip bone. It will take time, i.e. up to a year to recover and for the ligaments to strengthen.

Heart Diseases

Yorkies are prone to heart problems, such as a heart murmur caused by abnormal blood flow within the heart, usually associated with the heart valves.

Symptoms: Coughing, bluish tongue, lack of appetite, fatigue, heart beat that is too fast or too slow, increased effort in breathing.

Treatment: Drugs as prescribed by the vet may be given to the Yorkie. In conditions due to the heart muscle, nutrient supplements such as Carnitine, and Taurine are given as essential amino acids that may be deficient in some cases.

Cataracts

A condition that usually affects the senior dog but some younger as early as five years old get it too.

Symptoms: Cloudy eye balls, thick discharge, squinting or dull, dry eyes.

Treatment: Medication or surgery may be recommended, depending on the condition.

Kidney or Bladder Stones

Symptoms: Difficulty or inability to urinate or blood in the urine.

Treatment: Seek immediate attention from the vet when these symptoms are noticed. Surgery may be required to remove the stones.

Diseases Prevention

Though not all diseases in Yorkies can be prevented, we can help minimize the chances of your Yorkie to fall sick by ensuring the following:

i. Always give your Yorkie fresh water and wash its drinking dish daily before filling it up daily with fresh water.

ii. Avoid changing of a new diet too soon. Administer diet changes gradually and monitor your Yorkie's adaptability over time before its diet is changed completely.

iii. Have your Yorkie vaccinated annually or as per your vet's advice.

iv. Feed it with de-worming tablets once a quarter or as per your vet's advice.

v. Avoid feeding your Yorkie a diet than contains a high salt content.

5
Breeding

Recommended Age

A recommended age to commence breeding in female Yorkie is after her second heat, after 2 years of age and before she is 5 years old. Although a female Yorkie can enter heat when as young as 4 months old, it will still be too early and stressful for her body to go through pregnancy.

Beyond the age of 5, with 7 as the absolute limit, the female Yorkie's body may not be in her optimal state to carry the pregnancy. Depending on how many litters she has earlier had, it may be still possible to have her second and final litter at 7 years old. If she has had 3 or more litters prior to the age of 5, she should not conceive anymore beyond this age as it may lead to complications of the uterus or difficulty in delivery.

Recommended Weight

In achieving successful mating, it is essential note the sizes and weights of both the male and female Yorkies. The female should be heavier than the male, preferably in the range of 5 to 7 pounds so as to effectively carry the weight of the puppies and avoid complications in delivery. The weight of the male should not exceed 4 pounds or 1.81 kg.

As a responsible pet owner, you may like to check that both the male and female yorkies that you are pairing do not have any genetic issues so as to produce healthy offsprings that are free of health conditions that are inherited from their parents.

How to tell that your Yorkshire Terrier is on heat?

Often, the first sign in knowing if a female Yorkie is on its season is that the vulva will start to swell. This swelling can last for a week before bleeding is noticed. Apart from the swelling of the vulva, you may also notice changes in her behavior, such as licking her own body, a desire in getting on other dogs.

The most suitable time for her to mate would be able 12 days after the start of her bleeding, when the color of her blood faints off. If there is a male Yorkshire around, he will have a natural tendency to get near her from the distinctive smell that she gives out which male dogs will be attracted to during her heat season.

If the female and male Yorkies are interacting for the first time, it is essential to allow time for them to be familiarized with each other. Mutual attraction may not take place at times. If there are signs that the Yorkies are not showing liking for each other, they may end up aggressively attacking each other instead. You may wish to pair your Yorkie with another mate instead.

The female Yorkie will willingly let the male mount on her if she is receptive to mating with him. Human assistance may be required by gently holding on to the front body of the female to enable easier mating by the male Yorkie.

Yorkie Pregnancy Signs

As soon as your Yorkie is pregnant, you should be able to notice the following signs:

• Sleepiness and less active in her movements.
• Enlarged and protruding nipples
• Increase in appetite
• Some hardness in her stomach
• Enlarged abdomen after 3 weeks

A blood test at the vet after week 3 would accurately confirm if your Yorkie is pregnant. An ultrasound scan can be done by day 42 to determine the fetuses are growing normally.

Your Yorkie is likely gain about 1 to 2 pounds during her pregnancy. Each pregnancy can carry between 1 to 5 puppies, with an average of 4.

The average pregnancy would last for a duration for about 63 days. If your Yorkie has not delivered by day 67, it would be necessary to seek the help of a vet for assisted delivery.

Care for the Yorkie during pregnancy

Extra care and attention would need to be given to your Yorkie during her pregnancy. She will gradually be preparing her rest area to be her nest at the same time. It is hence essential for her to feel comfortable in this area that she is familiar with.

It is natural that your Yorkie's appetite will also increase as her pregnancy progresses. Do ensure that sufficient food is given to your Yorkie during this period. Exercising your Yorkie would help provide her with a healthy body for delivery. Keep the exercises to light ones such as slow walking and avoid jumping and excessive running.

If you are considering giving your Yorkie any supplements during her pregnancy, do consult the vet for advice.

By the 8th or 9th week, your Yorkie may not be behaving normally as these are likely symptoms that she is getting herself ready for delivery. You may like to lay in her nest area a comfortable towel with a pee sheet beneath it to prevent any stains from getting onto her resting bed/cushion. Ensure that her delivery space is large enough to fit herself and her puppies. She can then settle herself comfortably while awaiting her delivery.

You may like to bring her to a vet for delivery if this is new to you and you are not confident of handling it.

The labour and delivery process

The first signs of labour can be detected when your Yorkie's temperature drops to less than 100 degrees Fahrenheit. Her puppies are expected to be delivered within 24 hours. You will notice that she may be feeling uncomfortable as contractions may begin. She may also start to be seen attempting to push her puppies out.

It is advisable to have the following items ready to help your Yorkie in her delivery:

• Surgical gloves – To assist in the delivery process and carry the puppies.

• Infant's nasal aspirator/ bulk syringe – For suction of the puppies' mouth and nose if the sac has yet to be removed from the puppy.

• Dental floss – For tying the umbilical cord

• Iodine/Betadine – To promote healing

• Sharp Scissors – To cut the umbilical cord if needed

• Warm Towels – To gently rub the puppies after they are born.

When her water bag bursts, the Yorkie will start to push her puppies out in a sac one after another. The puppies can be born quickly one after another or up to two hours apart.

The head of the puppy would first appear in most instances. But if you are seeing the puppy' legs instead of its head from the opening of the vagina and your Yorkie is having difficulty in pushing it out, assist to pull it out gently in the direction of the curvature of the puppy's body.

The Yorkie will have a tendency to use her mouth in breaking open the sac as well as to detach the umbilical cord from her puppy. If the sac is still intact, you can break it by inserting the bulk syringe into the puppy's mouth and sucking the air out. You can remove the sac once it is open.

You can assist by tying the umbilical cord off about one inch from the puppy's body with a dental floss. Cut the umbilical cord a short distance from the knot with a pair of sharp scissors. Apply iodine or betadine at the end of the cord. Do not pull on the cord as it may hurt the puppy. The remaining cord should fall off in 2-3 days' time.

Rub the puppy with a warm and clean towel until you see that it starts to breathe, after which you can place it near its mother for her milk.

Feed the puppy milk from a bottle if it is unable to get enough milk from its mother due to overcrowding or inability to drink it directly from its mother.

Keep the nest clean by refreshing it with clean, old towels on a regular basis.

Note:

Bring your Yorkie to the vet immediately if:

i) Your Yorkie has not shown signs of labour beyond 70 days of pregnancy

ii) Your Yorkie has not delivered 24 hours after her temperature drops

iii) You are aware of more puppies inside but they are not coming out

iv) Your Yorkie is in severe pain

Care for your Yorkie and puppies post-delivery

Do ensure that your Yorkie is fed enough of nutritious food and plenty of water so as to produce a constant supply of milk for her puppies. The puppies would be fed on their mother's milk for the first 3 weeks. Wipe the Yorkie puppies with a warm towel to clean them as they would be too young to be showered.

The puppies should visit the vet and receive their first de-worming if they meet the weight and health requirements at 3 weeks.

Weaning can start at 4 weeks where solid food can be gradually introduced. Simple house training can also commence to get the puppies familiarized with the rules.

The second de-worming can be around 5 weeks, upon the approval of the vet.

At 6 weeks, more solid food can be introduced as your Yorkie may be producing much lesser milk by this time. You can start to bathe and groom your Yorkie puppies from this time.

The puppies should also receive their first vaccinations from the vet for common diseases like Hepatitis, Coronavirus, Distemper, Parvovirus and

Parainfluenza.

6
Spaying and Neutering

Benefits of spaying and neutering

Spaying is a term used for the sterilization for female animals where their uterus and ovaries will be removed via surgery. Neutering is the equivalent term for male animals where their testicles will be removed.

While the natural intent of sterilizing a dog is to prevent it from mating, another practical reason would be for the prevention of diseases associated with its reproductive organs, such as infections and cancer. The risk of contracting such diseases will increase with age. This applies to both female and male dogs. The following are some common diseases of the reproductive organs of the female and male dogs:

<u>Male dogs</u>
• Testicular infections
• Testicular tumours
• Enlargement of the prostate - may lead to urinary and rectal blockage and problems
• Prostate cancer
• Disorders of the prepuce (foreskin)

<u>Female dogs</u>
• Ovarian infections
• Ovarian cancer
• Inflammation of the uterus
• Pyometra disease – infection of the uterus resulting from enlarged glands and endometrium.
• Vaginitis - inflammation of the vagina
• Vagina tumours
• Disorders of the mammary (milk production) glands – e.g. inflammation and tumours

In the case of a female dog, an additional reason is to prevent any prevent any pregnancies beyond the age of 8 as this would pose a high risk to her health if she was to conceive at this age or older.

Recommended age

The recommended age for the sterilization of a dog would be as young as 6 months, or before a female dog experiences her first heat if you have no plans for her to mate. The chances of a female dog in developing mammary cancer increases with each heat cycle. It is advisable for spaying or neutering of your Yorkie to be done no later than the age of 5 as the health risks of your dog greatly increases by then. Not only will the costs of surgery be more expensive beyond this age, the risks of any complication for your dog to undergo general anesthesia may also be higher with an increase in age.

It is hence ideal for sterilization to be done as soon as possible for your dog as every delay will expose your dog to the health risks that are related to their reproductive system. An unsterilized dog may be affected by hormone changes if it has other medical conditions like diabetes.

Will spaying or neutering affect my Yorkie's personality or behaviour?

Spaying or neutering of your Yorkie will only affect behavior that is related to its sex hormones. Behavioural changes that you are likely to be observed would be as follows:

• Less urine marking

• Aggressive behavior as a result of reduction of testosterone

• Reduction in desire to mount on other dogs

• Elimination of anxiety or irritability associated with each cycle of her ovulation.

Spaying or neutering will not affect your dog's natural personality like playfulness, friendliness and its normal capabilities to function.

7

The Senior Years

Signs of aging

Small dogs like Yorkshire Terriers tend to have a longer lifespan than larger dogs. The following is a reference in finding the human age equivalent based on a Yorkie's age.

2 Yorkie years : 24 Human years

3 Yorkie years : 28 Human years

4 Yorkie years : 32 Human years

5 Yorkie years : 36 Human years

6 Yorkie years : 40 Human years

7 Yorkie years : 44 Human years

8 Yorkie years : 48 Human years

9 Yorkie years : 52 Human years

10 Yorkie years : 56 Human years

11 Yorkie years : 60 Human years

12 Yorkie years : 64 Human years

13 Yorkie years : 68 Human years

14 Yorkie years : 72 Human years

15 Yorkie years : 76 Human years

16 Yorkie years : 80 Human years

17 Yorkie Years : 84 Human years

A yorkie is considered a senior dog when it is 8 years or older. However, the health of each dog would differ and some may still be fit and in the pinkest of health even at this age.

An obvious sign to know if your Yorkie's body has advanced to its senior years is from the speed of its running. Your Yorkie may not be running as fast as before or it may become more challenging for it to jump up or down the bed or sofa. You may also your Yorkie sleeping or lying down more often.

Tooth decay is common if its teeth have not been cleaned regularly. It would be helpful to bring your Yorkie for a dental treatment where it will be put under general anesthesia. Decayed tooth will be extracted and scaling of the remaining teeth can be done for your Yorkie at the same time.

The lens of your Yorkie's eyes may look greyish instead of the black that it used to have when it was young. Do check for any cloudy film in its eyes as it be a symptom of cataracts. Your dog's vision may be affected as a result of cataracts and you may like to consider surgery to have the cataracts removed.

Your Yorkie's digestive system may also not be as strong as before. Vomiting or diarrhea may be seen more frequently.

Tiny growths or lumps may also be seen on its body. Most of them are benign cysts or fatty tumours that are harmless and can be left untreated. But if you were to notice that the lumps look irregular or sore, or having any discharge, accompanied by weight loss, bring them to a vet to have their conditions checked.

Other common medical conditions in senior Yorkies also include diabetes, arthritis, deterioration of sight and hearing, or even cancer.

Taking care of a senior Yorkie

Your Yorkie may require more frequent visits to the vet for checkups or treatments if needed based on its health condition.

You may like to gradually switch your Yorkie's diet to one that is suitable and nutritious for senior dog, such as one that is high in calcium. If your Yorkie has much of its teeth extracted, it may have difficulty chewing and digesting harder foods and you may like to provide him with a diet comprising softer foods as well as foods that have been cut to tiny pieces to make chewing and swallowing easier. Adding probiotics (usually in the form of a powder) to its food can help its digestive system and reduce the occurrences of vomiting or diarrhea due to problems with its digestive system.

Give it a bed that is comfortable and warm especially during the cold seasons as they may be suffering from joint discomfort or pain in its older years.

If your dog is suffering from a medical condition, do give it its needed dose of medication and take extra care in administering its diet.

If your Yorkie suffers from incontinence, you may wish to get them to wear nappies or disposable diapers for dogs to keep your place clean and maintain the hygiene of your dog.

Last but not least, remember to shower your Yorkie with lots of love and patience and be its companion throughout its senior years, just like it has given you a wonderful companionship in its younger days!

This book is dedicated to my lovely and playful Yorkie, Odie, 14 years old but still a puppy at heart!

www.ingramcontent.com/pod-product-compliance
Lightning Source LLC
Chambersburg PA
CBHW021409160726
47994CB00007B/3140